Volume 1

Tracing the Blue Economy

Awni Behnam

PUBLISHED BY THE FONDATION DE MALTE
Casa Cintraj 54, West Street, Valletta VLT 1536, Malta

SERIES EDITORS
DAVID RAPHAËL BUSUTTIL   SALVINO BUSUTTIL

© FONDATION DE MALTE 2013

This book is copyright. Subject to statutory exception and to provisions of relevant collective licensing agreements, no reproduction of any part may take place without the written permission of Fondation de Malte.

ISBN: 978-1-291-61589-0

The views expressed in the text pertain to their respective authors and do not necessarily reflect those of the Fondation de Malte which does not accept responsibility for remarks or comments expressed in any article, signed or unsigned, that appears in these pages.

E-mail: info@fondationdemalte.org
Web site: www.fondationdemalte.org

The Lumen Series

Fondation de Malte has, over the last seven years, published a successful series of publications, TELOS, where thematic discussions have spurred informed debate on issues which are topical, or on ideas which, as old as man, retain their contemporary relevance. In the same teleological search, Fondation now proposes to publish, from time to time, monographs on specific arguments.

For there spark, at times, inspirational thoughts which, often fleetingly but markedly, excite our imagination, challenging our spirit to reflection and action. Such moments may be enshrined in small niches, inviting the reader to further analysis.

Fondation de Malte feels that such auspicious mental initiatives call for early encapsulation lest their value, which is not ephemeral, loses its momentum. It is then in this setting that Fondation intends to publish such monographs.

Contributing to objective debate, they will not be academic exercises. Rather, they will seek to arouse interest in a given problematique. Discursive in tone, they will pose questions rather than identify final answers.

Shedding light on a particular concern, the monographs will be known as LUMEN (Latin for light).

The first monograph, TRACING THE BLUE ECONOMY, is an innovative essay by Awni Behnam, President of the International Ocean Institute and former Assistant Secretary-General of the United Nations.

Salvino Busuttil
President
Fondation de Malte
November 2013

Tracing the Blue Economy

A composite of presentations outlining the evolution of the concept:

"Living with the ocean and from the ocean in a sustainable relationship".

Awni Behnam

President, International Ocean Institute (I.O.I)

Former UN Assistant Secretary-General

Dedicated to the memory of

Elisabeth Mann Borgese

Mother of the Ocean

Acknowledgments

Tracing the Blue Economy is a composite paper of several presentations by the author made in response to invitations to:
- The Sixth Global Forum on Human Settlements, New York, USA; April 2011;
- The World Ocean Week, Xiamen, PR China; November 2011;
- The Global Forum on Electric Mobility and Conference on Sustainable Human Settlements, Rio, Brazil; June 2012;
- The East Asian Seas Congress, Changwon, Korea; July 2012;
- The Second APEC Blue Economy Forum, Tianjin, P. R. China; December, 2012;
- The World Urban Forum, Naples, Italy; September, 2012.

I wish to express my appreciation to the organisers of all the events listed above for the kind invitations extended to me to make presentations and keynote speeches at their fora.

I wish also to show my appreciation and gratitude for the assistance of Mary Chehab, a long-time colleague at UNCTAD and Antonella Vassallo, IOI OceanLearn Coordinator at IOIHQ in Malta, for their contribution to the organisation and editing of this manuscript. Finally, I wish to register my deep gratitude to Fondation de Malte which has generously agreed to publish this essay, as its first number in the LUMEN series.

Awni Behnam

Explanatory Note

The similarity of the title of this monograph referring to the "Blue Economy" to that of the Gunther Pauli in his book *"The Blue Economy: 10 years - 100 innovations - 100 million jobs"* (Paradigm Publications) is coincidental and the current monograph addresses the ocean and coastal interface specifically.

Contents

The Lumen Series 7
Tracing the Blue Economy 8
Acknowledgments 10
Executive Summary 14
PART ONE 27
    Human Settlements, Coasts and Ocean 32
    Ocean-urban Nexus Challenges 35
PART TWO 39
    Understanding the Concept of a Blue Economy 39
        Why the Blue Economy? 40
        Elements of a New Blue Economy Strategy 49
        (i)   Conformity of Short-term Action with Long-term Strategy. 50
        (ii)   National and International Measures 51
        (iii) Political and Economic Decision Making 52
        (iv) Demonstrating Commitments 52
        Partnerships 53
        Mobilizing National and International Public Opinion – the Societal Layer 53
    Demystifying the Blue Economy 54
        Is There a Role for the State in Managing the Blue Economy and for Multilateral Diplomacy for Governance? 55
        Does the Blue Economy Replace Accepted Ocean Governance Principles? 57
        Is the Blue Economy a Tool or a Process? 57
        Is the Blue Economy a Magic Wand? 59
        How are Communities and Property Protected in the Blue Economy ? 59

Is the Blue Economy a Licence for the Productive Sector to Exploit Resources with Impunity?..62
PART THREE **65**
What Has Changed and What Needs to Change: From UNCLOS to RIO+20 and the Ocean Compact..*65*
A Personal Reflection..*89*

Executive Summary

In 2007, at the flagship conference of the International Ocean Institute (IOI), *Pacem in Maribus* XXXII, held in Malta, the author coined the phrase *"living with the ocean and from the ocean in a sustainable relationship"*.[1] In 2010, *Pacem in Maribus* XXXIII was convened in China on the occasion of the World Expo 2010 in Shanghai. The conference – entitled *"Oceans, Climate Change and Sustainable Development: Challenges to Oceans and Coastal Cities"*, addressed the future challenges to coastal cities and the urban ocean nexus.[2] The debate on the ocean and urban interaction contributed to an emerging understanding of the Blue Economy paradigm.

The conference acknowledged that most urban centres are experiencing a fast and largely uncontrolled population growth, particularly in developing countries, that was more evident in coastal areas. The attraction of the seacoast since

---

[1] International Ocean Institute (IOI), Proceedings of Pacem in Maribus (PIM) XXXII, 2007, Malta. Drago A (ed). ISBN978-99932-06675
[2] IOI, Proceedings of PIM XXXIII, PR China 2010, *www.ioinst.org*

time immemorial as an ideal site for human settlement has also been associated with the link to original evolution of life from the sea which creates a profound link with humans and settlements. Settling along large bodies of water such as seas, lakes and rivers has historically been a vital factor in the economic and demographic growth of cities. Today 75 percent of mega cities with populations over ten million are located in coastal zones.[3]

Currently about 2.8 billion people (more than 40 percent of total global population) live and work in coastal cities. There is no doubt that the current deterioration of the health of the ocean is in large part due to the result of human settlement behaviour and resource exploitation patterns and their negative impact on the marine and coastal ecosystems. The Millennium Ecosystem Assessment, called for by the United Nations Secretary-General Kofi Annan in 2000, indicated strongly that marine and coastal ecosystems providing essential services to humankind are at the same time the most threatened.[4]

---

[3] World Ocean Review (WOR 1) 2010; http://worldoceanreview.com/en/

[4] The Millennium Ecosystem Assessment (MA) was called for by the United Nations Secretary-General Kofi Annan in 2000. More

Beyond the heavy legacy of human neglect of the health of the ocean and the role it plays in the very survival of our species and despite a long list of international laws and legal and voluntary instruments beginning with UNCLOS,[5] humans have failed miserably to protect both ocean and coast. There is no doubt about human's failure to *live with ocean and from the ocean in a sustainable relationship.*

In addition, new and emerging challenges such as climate change, repetitive financial and economic crises and security considerations (both economic and social)[6] are forcing a paradigm shift in the governance required at the ocean-urban nexus and a redefinition of human relations with ocean and coast.

The interconnectedness of emerging global challenges is forcing a policy dimension change in

---

information regarding the Millennium Ecosystem Assessment is available on *http://www.unep.org/maweb/en/index.aspx* (accessed 16 May 2013)

[5] UN Convention on the Law of the Sea, New York, 2001, ISBN 22-1-133522-1

[6] Water: Preserving our Oceans, IPU, Concept Paper 122nd Assembly, Bangkok, Thailand; 27th March - 1st April 2010, Page 14

the form of the **Blue Economy** because of the complex and interlinked temporal and spatial impacts on the oceans and seas and the urban hinterland, where humans have to adapt to *living with the ocean and from the ocean in a sustainable relationship*. This relationship is to be understood as an incorporation of two opposing directions; that of making sustainable use of the abundant goods and services of the ocean and that of the mitigation and adaptation to dangers the ocean presents to prosperity and human well-being.

The Blue Economy paradigm may be explained as an integrated approach to the governance of the ocean and urban interface, revolving around the human dimension. The paradigm implies that there is an inclusive partnership between all stakeholders that internalizes the conformity of the short term needs with long term objectives of sustainability.

The two most immediate challenges that are being addressed are the major impact of climate change and the consequence of sea-level rise to human settlements in the coastal zones. The Secretary-General of the United Nations, Mr Ban Ki-moon recalled in his message of 3 October 2011 that sixty million people live within one meter of the sea level.[7] The second challenge is the need for protection of human life and property from extreme weather and natural hazards including tsunamis. Clearly, for a way forward this calls for a changed mindset and governance tools including mitigation and adaptation measures, as well as behavioural change both in terms of attitudes toward ocean use and conservation and toward the protection of natural and human resources.

Living with the ocean and from the ocean in prosperity and sustainability is a multi-dimensional and interdependent responsibility of all stake holders. While there is a clear need for collaborative scientific research and knowledge sharing with developing countries, it is also clear that the most disadvantaged, the least developed, the developing countries and economies in transition will require intensified capacity building and the provision of adequate financial resources in a timely and appropriate manner .

---

[7] United Nations Secretary-General Ban Ki-moon, United Nations Secretary-General's Message on UNHABITAT Day, 3 October 2011; *http://www.unhabitat.org/content.asp?cid=10290 &catid=669&typeid=8&subMenuId=0;* (accessed 17 May 2013);

The traditional approach to sustainable development remains the basis of the Green Economy - a land-locked vision that looked from land to the ocean space as if it were an endless horizon with limitless resources. The paradigm shift came when Elisabeth Mann Borgese – founder of the International Ocean Institute – viewed the situation from the seaward side, where a sustainable ocean economy integrates with and is inclusive of the Green Economy. She famously stated *"if before you saw the sea and the sea floor as a continuation of the land, you now see the land as a continuation of the sea,"*[8]. The concept of the Blue Economy is an attempt to do justice to that genius vision.

Until now, contemporary wisdom has largely treated the ocean as a body of water isolated from the coast and hinterland in terms of an integrated whole of socio-economic, environmental and physical attributes of sustainability. The prevailing paradigm in ocean governance addresses ocean and coastal interaction mainly from the impact of humans on the use and exploitation of ocean services and resources (*living from the ocean*).

---

[8] Elizabeth Mann Borgese, Oceanic Circle UNV Press 1998 NY, ISBN 92-808-1028-6, page 4;

Consequently the Blue Economy is a concept derived from the fact that we live on a planet made of up to 75 percent of ocean. When examining this with our "land based" vision what we see is basically limited to an ocean and coast interface. But the economy of this planet must be seen as an integrated whole and in homage to our blue planet we can call it "The Blue Economy" which in essence implies the full interaction of the human species *"living with the ocean and from the ocean in a sustainable relationship"*.

In 2012 we celebrated the 30th anniversary of the opening for signature of the United Nations Convention of the Law of the Sea (UNCLOS). There is no doubt in our mind that it was one of humanity's great achievements to have adopted a universal constitution for the governance of oceans.

Unlike the *Mare Liberum* regime that dominated the governance of the oceans for centuries, UNCLOS was underpinned by an ethical and moral dimension based on the respect for common goods and it upheld the principle of the common heritage of humankind and the peaceful use of the ocean services and resources.

In the thirty years since the adoption of UNCLOS a plethora of complex governance architecture has developed in its support ranging from protocols, conventions, binding and non-binding multilateral agreements, guidelines, model rules etc. However, UNCLOS and all its related paraphernalia of instruments did not guarantee implementation and compliance. Our oceans are in deep trouble despite all the good intentions and good will expressed by all stake holders. The human imprint on the ocean has been destructive and unconscionable. At the same time nations have failed to protect property and life from the might and majesty of the oceans' natural impact on humans and their property and settlements, an impact that has been further aggravated by humankind's effect on climate.

Since the adoption of UNCLOS, a stark governance deficit has evolved in terms of the sustainability of humankind's interaction with the oceans. Thirty years since the adoption of the sole constitution of the ocean, time-advances in knowledge and innovation have created an additional burden on implementation to add to the systemic issues that remained unresolved in UNCLOS - such as the scope of application of the common heritage principle, effective exercise of flag state duties and jurisdiction in the absence of the genuine link, as well as the lack of clarity in the application of rule of law in areas beyond national jurisdiction on the high seas.

The deteriorating health of the oceans, the overexploitation of its living resources and the irreparable damage to its biodiversity and the new and emerging challenges of climate change were on the minds of many concerned stakeholders as Rio+20: "the summit on Sustainable Development"[9] approached in 2012. Much was at stake and there were many expectations including those linking the Blue Economy to the sustainable development of ocean and coasts.

As a new concept, born out of the 2010 IOI *Pacem in Maribus XXXIII* conference in Beijing, the Blue Economy may not have been well understood. Much hope was placed in Rio+20 by the ocean community. Also, for the first time in twenty years, the ocean was on the agenda of international multilateral negotiations in terms of sustainable

---

[9] Rio+20 is the name given to the UN Conference on Sustainable Development, held in 2012, to commemorate the 20th anniversary of the first Earth Summit of 1992 held in Rio de Janeiro, Brazil;

development. While Rio+20 fell short of the aspirations of the ocean community it was nevertheless encouraging that not only the commitments to UNCLOS but also to other related instruments were reconfirmed by Member States. However Rio+20 was silent on some of the most urgent challenges.

The outcome of Rio+20[10] was, the setting-up, within two months, of a major initiative of Mr Ban Ki–moon, United Nations Secretary-General, who launched his comprehensive Oceans Compact on 12 August 2012.-[11]

The stated aim of the Oceans Compact initiative of the UNSG is to set out a strategic vision for the UN system to deliver on its ocean related mandates, consistent with the Rio+20 outcome, in a more

---

[10] The Future We Want, outcome document of Rio+20, GA (A/66/L.56) NY, 24 July 2012;

[11] The Oceans Compact, Healthy Oceans for Prosperity. An initiative of the United Nations Secretary-General, 2012, *www.un.org*; *https://www.un.org/Depts/los/ ocean_compact/oceans_compact.htm;* (accessed 17 May 2013) *Oceans Compact: On 12 August 2012, at the Yeosu (Republic of Korea) International Conference to commemorate the thirtieth anniversary of the opening for signature of the United Nations Convention on the Law of the Sea, the United Nations Secretary-General, Mr Ban Ki-moon, launched the Oceans Compact – an initiative to strengthen United Nations system-wide coherence to deliver on its oceans-related mandates.*

coherent manner and to aim to provide a platform for all stakeholders to collaborate and accelerate progress in the achievement of the common goal of Healthy Oceans for Prosperity. It is expected to build upon the range of existing and ongoing activities of the UN organizations to assist member States to implement UNCLOS and other relevant global and regional conventions.

The first observation on this Compact initiative is its emphasis on the implementation of UNCLOS and the fact that it up-scales commitments of member states and recommits the United Nations System with a new mechanism for follow-up and cooperation.

The second is that it comes ever so close to the Blue Economy concept of *"living from the ocean and with the ocean in a sustainable relationship"* as it addresses the nexus of ocean and coast and the protection of life and property. The very first of the Compact's three goals and objectives is the protection of people and the improvement of the health of the ocean, while Rio+20 focused to a larger part on the living resources of the ocean.

Will the combination of these two approaches suffice to change the *status quo* for a new international consensus to meet the ever urgent challenges of humanity? The survival of our kind on this blue planet will depend on all of the stake holders and to the extent that every individual assumes his or her responsibility and accepts a share in the inevitable sacrifices to be made.

PART ONE

Towards Understanding the Concept of the Blue Economy: The Ocean Urban Nexus

In 2010, a remarkable experience unfolded in the shape of the Shanghai World Expo 2010.[1] Four years in the preparation and planned under the theme *"Better City, Better Life"*, it was designed to be the most successful World Expo ever. UNHABITAT's leadership for the United Nations' pavilion was secured by the United Nations Secretary-General and the author was appointed in 2008 as the Commissioner General for the UN Pavilion.

The UN's presence at the Shanghai World Expo 2010 was an extension of the core values that underpin the work and the core values of the United Nations and one could not envisage the absence of the UN's role in such a global experiment in international cooperation and exchange of cultures. The World Expo proved to be a most coherent tool to conduct a dialogue of cultures as it mobilized all the human senses in a cultural interaction of the total sum of humanity. It provided a magical capsule in space and time to bring out the wealth and richness of diversity in the service of humanity.

The Expo helped the international community to learn not to fear differences or to jealously guard achievements, but to share and support the common goal of achieving an equitable and sustainable progress of individuals and society. With its theme of *"Better City, Better Life"*, it was an exceptional opportunity for such an international engagement.

The full and proactive engagement of the UN was in itself demonstrative of the importance of the Expo's contribution to world peace and sustainable development as it provided a special moment in history for an effective and beneficial exchange of knowledge, best practices and solutions developed by communities, societies and nations on this our unique planet.

The Secretary-General of the United Nations, Mr Ban Ki-moon, decided on the theme *"One Earth, One UN"* to reflect the organization's united efforts

---

[1] Shanghai World Expo 2010, *www.expo2010.cn*;

towards building economically, socially and environmentally sustainable cities. The theme of one earth is centred on the inescapable fact that we all have to share this one planet in a sustainable relationship as we go forward in preparing for better cities and better lives. Consequently, an overarching concept of the role of sustainable development became central to the concept of the Pavilion.[2]

The Expo was an opportunity for mass outreach and outdid all other communication tools and strategies as it provided for a close personal experience of humanity's interaction. Its intangibles and related benefits could not be underestimated particularly in promoting awareness. It was a virtual crucible of the United Nations where all nations put forward their best aspirations and expressed their

---

[2] The UN Pavilion showcased the great urban challenges facing developed and developing countries, such as urban poverty and climate change, the greening of cities, challenges to coastal cities as well as new ideas, solutions and actions taken by various UN agencies and their partners to build better cities and better living conditions and that would contribute to meeting the Millennium Development Goals (MDGs). [The Millennium Development Goals (MDGs) are eight international goals established by the UN Millennium Summit in 2000, *www.un.org/millenniumgoals]*
The dazzling, state-of-the-art UN Pavilion attracted 3.5 million visitors. Indeed, thousands of people queued for hours every day to get a glimpse of what the UN does and how it works.

own policies and strategies in meeting the global challenges for *"Better City, Better Life"*.³

Thus, some realities came into play, one of which is the relevance of the Ocean/Urban interface. Conventional wisdom has largely treated the ocean

---

³ A very special feature of the Expo were the six thematic forums which took place with a lead UN agency including the World Bank and counterpart ministries from China. The thematic forums varied from Information and Urban Development (ITU); Cultural Heritage and Urban Regionalization (UNESCO); Science Innovation and Urban Future (UNCTAD); Towards a Low Carbon City: Urban Responsibilities and Environment (UNEP); Economic Transformation, Urban and Rural Interaction (World Bank); Liveable City in a Harmonious Society (UNHABITAT); and The Summit Forum (UNDESA) which adopted the Shanghai Declaration.

In addition, there was the contribution of individual pavilions in terms of events and exhibits aimed at expanding awareness of physical and social solutions to urban sustainability through visitors experiencing physical and practical solutions, ideas and innovation. The result has been an accumulation of wealth of knowledge in the intellectual bank of the Expo. At these interactions I was asked often what a future city could be like. [Behnam A. UNHABITAT, Urban World, Volume 2, issue 4 September 2010]

My response to the question was that a future city is a fair city that is inclusive, where all find in it equal opportunities and services without discrimination. A future city is one whose governance is in the hands of all stakeholders who share in the decision-making, where local communities have a voice in their governance. A future city is also one that protects cultural heritage and does not divorce itself from the traditional past while it enriches modernity through cultural diversity and creativity, a future city is one that invests in the potential and expectations of its youth and facilitates their empowerment. A future city is one that does not distance itself and its communities from its rural roots where modern cities remain closely linked with the values of rural life despite rapid urban development. However, that must go together with a capacity to protect life and property which accordingly should be made possible and feasible.

as a body of water isolated from the coast and hinterland in terms of an integrated whole of socio-economic, environmental and physical attributes of sustainability. The prevailing paradigm in ocean governance addresses ocean and coastal interaction mainly from the impact of humans on the use and exploitation of ocean services and resources (*living from the ocean*).

For that reason the International Ocean Institute convened during the Shanghai World EXPO its flagship conference *Pacem in Maribus* (Peace in the Oceans) in Beijing and Shanghai. The theme of the PIMXXXIII Conference was *"Oceans, Climate Change and Sustainable development: Challenges to Oceans and Coastal Cities.* The focus was specifically on the future challenges to coastal cities.[4]

The selection of that theme came from the realization of the importance that the mutual impact of the ocean and the urban coast has on the economic, social and environmental sustainability of the coast and hinterland. Coastal cities are the epicentres of the ocean-land interaction. In that context the conference drew attention to the ocean and the interdependent relationship between oceans, coasts and humans that inhabit the coast. Consequently the Ocean–Urban Nexus was under scrutiny.

Human Settlements, Coasts and Ocean

Most urban centres are experiencing a fast and largely uncontrolled population growth, particularly in developing countries. This has been more evident in coastal areas. The attraction of the seacoast since time immemorial as an ideal site for human settlement has also been associated with the link to original evolution of life from the sea which creates a profound link with humans and settlements. Settling along large bodies of water such as seas, lakes and rivers has historically been a vital factor in the economic and demographic growth of cities. Today 75 percent of the mega cities with populations over ten million are located in coastal zones.[5]

---

[4] IOI, Proceedings PIM XXXIII, Shanghai 2010, *www.ioinst.org*;
[5] WOR 1, 2010 (*opcit*), page 60;

The coastal zone is the interface between land, ocean and atmosphere. The World Ocean Review (WOR) explains that the coastal zone encompasses an area where the land is significantly influenced by the sea and the sea is notably influenced by the land, a complex place that is equally influenced by human activity. Coastal zones cover 20 percent of the earth space, where more than 45 percent of the population live and work. It is growing faster than any other region on the planet. In fact, coastal cities have higher densities than inland cities and are growing faster than inland cities.[6]

The concern lies in the magnitude of the interdependent impact that the nexus between ocean and urban coast and human settlement has on the economic, social and environmental sustainability of ocean and coast. Coastal cities are at the front line of this impact.

All observations and scientific evidence to date point to a devastating effect of humans on the health of the ocean and the sustainability of its ecosystem, resources and services. The damage does not necessarily begin with human settlements on the coast. For example, in many regions, sedimentary

---

[6] *Ibid*, page 63;

replenishment of the coastline is triggered by a paucity of sediments which can be traced to modifications of the coastline and inland structures created through human intervention. Therefore the worldwide existence of over 41,000 large dams, and many more smaller ones, have been responsible for the blockage of about 14 percent of total global sediment flow, causing severe losses of sediment flows often compounded by the damage engendered by human settlement growth rates and coastal modifications and encouraging land reclamation from the ocean. When the constant flow of land based pollution is added to this, the damage to the biotic environment can easily become irreversible.

Coastal settlements, while providing untold economic opportunities for the settlers, in return require that humans have to ensure a sustainable relationship with both the coast and ocean. While this is easily said, in practice, the challenge is enormous.[7]

---

[7] *Ibid*, page 63-68;

Ocean-urban Nexus Challenges

Let us recall briefly that sixty million people now live within one meter of the sea level. By the end of this century, that number is expected to jump to 130 million. By 2025, about 75 percent of the world's population could be living within 100 km of its coasts.[8]

Our planet ocean is one and no person or place is insulated or isolated - we are all interconnected. Confucius brilliantly described our universality *"if a man takes no thought about what is far off, he will find troubles near at home."*[9] It is true that under the UNCLOS governance architecture we have imaginary boundaries, territorial waters, contiguous zones, exclusive economic zones, continental shelves and high seas, however, to take one example, any port manager - no matter where geographically situated on the planet - must be prepared to deal with the challenges of invasive species or sea level rise. In the Blue Economy there is an acceptance of

---

[8] UNSG message World Habitat Day 2011 (*opcit*);
[9] Confucius said *"if a man takes no thought about what is far off, he will find troubles near at home."* The Confucius Analects, Chinese philosopher and reformer (551 BC – 497 BC);

the natural interdependence of every entity: local, sub-regional, regional, inter-regional and international. In one form or other every single stakeholder impacts on others and vice versa. Therefore, all stakeholders are obliged to act locally but must prepare to meet challenges of international origin.

Today more than 2.8 billion people (over 40 percent of the total global population) live and work in coastal cities within 100km of the coast.[10] There is no doubt that the current deterioration of the health of the ocean is in large part due to the result of the pressures exerted by human settlement and the negative impact on the oceans and coasts ecosystems. The Millennium Ecosystem Assessment - called for by the UNSG for the year 2000[11] - indicated strongly that marine and coastal ecosystems providing essential services to humankind are the most threatened.

---

[10] from Rio+20 Facts and Figures : *http://www.unwomen.org/the-united-nations-conference-on-sustainable-development-rio20/facts-and-figures/*: *"More than 40 per cent of the world's population (more than 2.8 billion people) live within 100 kilometres of the coast. Rapid urbanization will lead to more coastal mega-cities containing 10 million or more people. Thirteen of the world's 20 megacities lie along coasts and nearly 700 million people live in low lying coastal areas less than ten meters above sea level."*

[11] *http://www.unep.org/maweb/en/index.aspx*

Beyond the heavy legacy of human neglect of the health of the ocean and the role it plays in the very survival of our species and despite a long list of international laws and legal and voluntary instruments, beginning with UNCLOS, humans have failed miserably to protect the ocean and coast. There is no doubt about human's failure to *live with ocean and from the ocean in sustainable relationship.*

In addition, new and emerging challenges such as climate change, repetitive financial and economic crises and security considerations (economic and social) combined with a governance deficit are forcing a paradigm shift in the governance of the ocean-urban nexus and a redefinition of human relations with ocean and coast.

The interconnectedness of emerging global challenges is forcing a policy dimension change due to their complex and interlinked temporal and spatial impacts on the ocean and the urban hinterland in the form of the an **integrated (Blue) economy, in contrast to a marine economy or an urban economy.** In this shift of policy dimension, humans will have to adapt to *living with the ocean, and from the ocean, in a sustainable relationship.* This relationship is to be understood as an incorporation of two opposing directions; that of making sustainable use of the abundant goods and services of the ocean, and that of adaptation to and mitigation of the dangers the ocean presents to prosperity and human well-being.

The Blue Economy paradigm is an integrated approach to the governance of the ocean and urban interface, revolving around the human dimension. The paradigm implies that there is an inclusive partnership between all stakeholders that internalizes the conformity of the short term needs with long term objectives of sustainability.

PART TWO

Understanding the Concept of a Blue Economy

The Blue Economy is a concept derived from the fact that we live on one planet made of up to 75 percent of ocean, with a minor percentage of land mass. When seeing this with our land based vision what we see is basically an ocean and coast interface. But the economy of this planet must be seen as an integrated whole and as homage to our blue planet we can call it the "Blue Economy" in essence implying the full interaction of the human species *living with the ocean and from the ocean in a sustainable relationship.*

This concept is understood intuitively and is not defined in a legal sense. It is a state of mind which should be translated into action. Put simply and in the words of Victor Hugo *"nothing is as powerful as an idea whose time has come";* as we increasingly recognize the interdependence of all elements in the interaction between humans, land and ocean.

Why the Blue Economy?

The Blue Economy defined as *living with the ocean and from the ocean in a sustainable relationship,* is the transition toward a human-ocean centred relationship where humankind coexists with the ocean and from the ocean in a sustainable way. It is also understood that the concept of Blue Economy integrates two dimensions – that of the provision of goods and services and the protection and security of property and life in a manner which is sustainable and guarantees the rights of future generations.

On the one hand, the ocean offers apparently limitless services essential for the survival and prosperity of humans – in fields ranging from recreation to research, from travel to trade, from food to medicine, from waste disposal to carbon sink, from energy to minerals, from climate control to border control and much, much more. At the same time the ocean follows laws of nature far beyond human control and the oceans can be devastating in their might. From this, humankind has always sought deliverance or protection through resilience, avoidance, mitigation and adaptation. Recent tsunamis, hurricanes, cyclones, storm surges, extreme coastal weather events, and other marine hazards are in the majority not triggered by human activities. Of course, anthropogenic sources of climate change could be said to exacerbate and worsen some of these phenomena - hence the need for individuals and communities to protect themselves from these phenomena and become more climate resilient to climatic changes and hazards.

In this relationship of *living with the ocean and from the ocean,* humans need to learn and find innovative ways and means of responding with preparedness, adaptation and mitigation measures of which the costs and benefits are an integral component of the economy as a whole.

Application of this concept fully is essential to any country's wealth, growth, prosperity and sustainable development. A large number of countries are dependent on the contribution to the Gross Domestic Product (GDP) of activities in their coastal areas (shipping, tourism, fisheries, aquaculture, energy, national defence, etc.). All these factors have to be integrated into holistic and collective governance architecture just as their value added is interconnected. The emerging Blue Economy may be characterized by the integration and acknowledged interdependence of all stakeholders and actors and thus calls for a different type of strategy and governance. Nowhere is this more urgent than in addressing one of the greatest challenges of our time, namely that proposed by a changing climate and the implications to the ocean-urban nexus.

Currently the benefits derived from the sustainable use of ocean services and resources do not reflect the socioeconomic dimensions of an ocean-urban nexus economy so the true value of human interaction and wellbeing, derived from and because of the ocean, is never quantified, internalized or incorporated into the fiscal and investment policies, whether national or local.

The Blue Economy renders imperative an inclusive stakeholder participation in collaborative governance based on linkages between ocean, coastal and urban systems that internalizes the vulnerability of communities and infrastructure. In the Blue Economy there would be a need to quantify internal benefits of different activities and the commensurate viable socio-economic contribution to resilience through preparedness, mitigation and adaptation by the nation or community.

The Blue Economy at the national level revolves around an efficient and sustainable use of ocean and coastal services and resources that internalizes external costs together with an efficient valuing of natural non-market assets and services and the access thereto. This however makes imperative a major reform of the financial architecture governance for a fiscal overhaul that reflects all aspects of ocean services.

An important tenet of the Blue Economy is that the responsibility as well as sharing in the costs and benefits does not rest with one entity such as the State but it should be spread among all stake holders. It is the responsibility of all stake holders in a holistic model, at the level of the individual, the locality, the community, the society, the region, the national level and the international, public and particularly private sectors.

Let us recall that by the year 2025 about 75 percent of the world population could be living within 100 km of the coast. With the ocean providing services close to US$32 trillion[1] in areas

---

[1] Oceans: The Source of Life: United Nations Convention on the Law of the Sea - 20th Anniversary (1982-2002) by UNDOALOS (UN-NY-

such as the provision of living and non-living resources, transportation (ninety percent of world trade moves by sea),[2] communication, recreation, energy production, waste disposal, medicinal goods, marine genetic resources etc., there is increased potential for discovery and exploitation of many more services as we learn more about the oceans. Based on the extent of the sustainable use of services provided by the ocean, the Blue Economy will also become an issue of security and intergenerational equity.

Regrettably, however, the human impact on the ocean, through use and exploitation, has been destructive and unconscionable because humans have taken for granted the sustainability of the ocean. In so doing, and despite decades of efforts to evolve an adequate governance regime, the ocean's fragile ecosystems are being systematically destroyed.

2002).
http://www.un.org/Depts/los/convention_agreements/convention_20year s/oceanssourceoflife.pdf (accessed 20 May 2013); See also Costanza et al: The value of the World's Ecosystem Services and Natural Capital in NATURE |VOL 387 | 15 MAY 1997

[2] United Nations Secretary-General, the Oceans Compact, Initiative of the UN Secretary-General, July 2012, *www.un.org/depts/los/oceans compact*, page 2

Environmental damage is ongoing in the form of land-based and seaborne pollution; over-exploitation and depletion of its living and non-living resources, loss of biodiversity and destructive human practices, such as in coastal development; fisheries; climate change and the acidification of the ocean; sea-level rise and coastal flooding; destruction of coral reefs, mangroves and wetlands; habitat loss; deforestation and changes in hydrology, turbidity, sedimentation; mineral, sand and gravel extraction. All this suggest that the *status quo* is not tenable and there exists a major governance failure on behalf of humanity.

The Beijing Declaration[3] was very clear on the future challenges to coastal cities. It emphasized the need for a long term perspective in management of coastal cities that integrate the four components of environment, economy, culture and society. A Blue Economy ecosystem management renders imperative an inclusive stakeholder participation in collaborative governance based on linkages between coastal and urban systems that internalizes the vulnerability of the urban/coastal community and infrastructure.

Climate Change is placing increasing pressure on coastal regions which are already seriously affected by intensive human activity. This raises the question as to the extent that these areas will retain their residential and economic value in the decades and centuries to come or whether they instead may pose a threat to the human race, one undeniable threat being that from sea level rise. The Secretary-General of the UN on 3 October 2011[4] stated:

"Rising sea levels are major impact of climate change and an urgent concern. Sixty million people now live within one meter of sea level by the end of the century the number will jump to 130 million. Major coastal cites – such as Cairo, New York, Karachi, Calcutta, Belem, New Orleans, Shanghai, Tokyo, Lagos, Miami, and Amsterdam – could face serious threats from storm surges. The nexus between urbanization and climate change is real and potentially deadly".

The first World Ocean Review[5] lists the following five effects of sea-level rise on the natural coastal system: sea level rise, flooding, loss of coastal

---

[3] IOI Proceedings of PIM XXXIII (*opcit*);
[4] United Nations Secretary-General Message, World Habitat Day 2011, (*opcit*);
[5] IOI, WOR 1, 2010, *www.worldoceanreview.com/en/*;

wetlands, erosion of beaches and bluffs, intrusion of saltwater and limited soil drainage. So in addition to the impact of intensive and damaging human activities at the coast, climate change compounds the situation. Just as the melting of the polar ice due to global warming will undermine the buffer effect provided by sea ice on coasts in polar and sub-polar regions, coasts will therefore be subjected not only to rising water levels but also to extreme weather events such as storms and storm surges.

Reducing the vulnerabilities of people in coastal settlements must be the first priority in many countries, particularly developing countries where informal coastal settlements are often the first victims of hazards either of natural origin such as tsunamis or anthropogenically induced.

The World Ocean Review[6] warns that *"without doubt sea level will rise slowly at first, speeding up and continuing beyond the 21st century. Gradually many coastal areas will become uninhabitable. People will lose their homes and part of their culture"*. According to the same report more than one billion people, most of them in Asia, are threatened. Such population displacement is a recipe for conflict and a threat to global security.

Currently the benefits derived from the sustainable use of ocean services and resources do not reflect the socioeconomic dimensions of an ocean-urban economy so the true value of human interaction and wellbeing derived from and with the ocean is never quantified or internalized and incorporated into the fiscal and investment policies at the national level.

The Blue Economy at the national level revolves around efficient and sustainable use of ocean and coastal services and resources that internalizes external costs together with an efficient valuing of natural non-market assets and services and the access thereto. This however makes imperative a major reform of the financial architecture for a fiscal overhaul that reflects all aspects of ocean services.

---

[6] World Ocean Review 1, *ibid.*;

An important tenet of the Blue Economy is that the responsibility as well as sharing in the cost and benefits does not rest with one entity such as the State but is spread among all stake holders. It is the responsibility of all stake holders in an integrated paradigm at the level of the individual, child and adult, the locality, the community, the society, the region, the national and the international level, the public and private sectors. Thus it may be stated that the Blue Economy is a proactive concept and implies adopting and implementing corrective measures combined with the allocation of adequate resources; in comparison the *Marine Economy* focuses principally on the costs and benefits of ocean services and resources.

Elements of a New Blue Economy Strategy

In formulating their strategies of *living with the ocean and from the ocean in a sustainable relationship* most developing countries have had to start from a shallow base lacking in the necessary safety nets and fundamental necessities to meet the conditionality of integrated and comprehensive ocean and coast policies and related governance. It is also pertinent to recall in the context of the Blue Economy that ocean governance and terrestrial governance are part of one system where the costs and benefits are internalized. Thus, there is also a need to align the national policies with regional and global imperatives by accommodating the following factors:[7]

(i) Conformity of Short-term Action with Long-term Strategy

This refers *inter alia* to investment. It is often necessary to make short-term investment and appropriate adjustment in marine infrastructure systems in any one sector or discipline. However, short term financing which is aimed at dispersing a bottleneck or an immediate need should be identified as part of the long-term investment strategy in the development of any specific sector. Thus, adjustments, which are made to ameliorate a specific immediate situation should support the

---

[7] Behnam A., "Issues for Implementing National and Regional Ocean Policies"; Presentation by the Chair during TOPS 2005: The Ocean Policy Summit: International Conference on Integrated Ocean Policy: National and Regional Experiences, Prospects, and Emerging Practices; October 10-14, 2005, Lisbon, Portugal. Organised by the Global Forum on Oceans, Coasts and Islands.
http://www.globaloceans.org/content/ocean-policy-summit-2005 (accessed 20 May 2013);

achievement of long-term targets (e.g. artisanal fishing, intensive fishing and sustainability of living resources; compatibility of domestic and international tourism; upgrading from multipurpose to specialized ports and terminals etc.). Similarly, investment made in capacity building and on-the-job skills development should form part of more comprehensive, retooled and long-term view to train personnel, in other words a move to capacity development – **the individual layer.**

(ii) National and International Measures

In developing the policy framework, strategic links at the supranational level have to be carefully appraised. Currently, lack of coordination and joint planning between concerned neighbouring countries that share the same ocean space often leads to sub-optimal allocation of financial resources. While a pan-regional master plan cannot be imposed from the top, national plans need to be taken up to the "higher" level of regional and sub-regional for joint planning and investment in order to create the necessary linkages, synergies, coherence, and economies of scale.

(iii) Political and Economic Decision Making

A comprehensive strategy cuts across countries' boundaries. Its benefits are national as well as international. Unlike land-locked activities, it provides a nucleus for cooperation and creates a basis for joint effort at all levels of infrastructure: economic, physical, scientific, legal, environmental and ethical. Consider as an example early warning systems; to obtain the maximum advantage that can be reaped at the national, sub-regional, regional and consequently international level, it becomes necessary to demonstrate political will to an open policy of cooperation with the ultimate benefits of integration.

(iv) Demonstrating Commitments

Ratification of conventions, treaties and protocols in all the priority sectors identified is essential in order to benefit from technical and financial assistance that is available within the organizations of the United Nations system, the Bretton Woods Institutions, regional organizations and development banks and public funds. A demonstrative institutional commitment to the health of the ocean and the connected coast, and the sustainable use and protection of its resources combined with good governance encourages funders' positive attitudes – **the institutional layer**.

Partnerships

Strong partnerships between the private/public sectors attract international support, strengthen national commitments and mobilise resources. It is also conducive to adopting relevant policy space and promoting policy coherence. This is a **role for the productive layer**.

Mobilizing National and International Public Opinion – the Societal Layer

The personal experience of the author, with over thirty years service at the UN, suggests that even in the richest of countries the public have only superficial awareness of the importance of the impact of the ocean in their daily life let alone at the level of the planet. Strengthening a nations' awareness of the role played by oceans in its existence and the need to develop an integrated ocean and coastal policy through advocacy and education – formal and informal at all levels – is the gateway to the future. The engagement of civil society and partnerships with stakeholders plays a positive role in facilitating implementation and influencing public opinion. Empowering women, youth and coastal communities; engagement of the private sector, industry and non-governmental organizations as well as the scientific community in a framework of social responsibility will offer the necessary coherence for integrated policy implementation and can ensure harmony through **inclusiveness**.

Demystifying the Blue Economy

In contemplating the Blue Economy concept, one is reminded of chaos theory and E. N. Lorenz's description of dynamical systems posited to be highly sensitive to initial conditions, an effect which is popularly referred to as the "butterfly effect". On our blue planet everything is interlinked, interdependent and reactive to interaction whether economic, social, ecological or physical; as a result there is an innate contagion that often increases or decreases diversity thus affecting the *status quo* . It is the impact of the human species and its imprint on this planet as a global phenomenon that determines whether humankind moves along a sustainable curve or sinks into destruction.

Given today's realities, the concept of the Blue Economy calls for a systemic change from a behaviour based on economic values to one based on ethical and moral imperatives that promotes the respect for common goods and their sustainability as opposed to values of the market price and profit margins of production and exploitation that are driven by greed. Ensuring such ethical and moral economic values is dependent on an expressed governance architecture and an enlightened management that are necessary components of the concept.

Is There a Role for the State in Managing the Blue Economy and for Multilateral Diplomacy for Governance?

The answer is, of course, yes, because the Blue Economy is part and parcel of the future security of humankind. However, the Blue Economy is a concept and not an exact science. There exists no legal definition of the Blue Economy and it is unlikely that there will be a multilaterally agreed definition but we all understand intuitively the concept of *living with the ocean and from the ocean in a sustainable relation*. While as a concept it is not an exact science it can only be what it is by reliance on scientific knowledge and the effective integration of scientific knowledge in decision and policy making.

Hence, the economic parameters in the Blue Economy must, by deduction, be the long-term benefits from long-term investment which often has to be achieved at the pain of short-term cost and sacrifice. It is not about growth per se but it is about long term sustainable growth and quality of life. It should be about a balance between growth in services and resource use and the quality of life of people and coastal communities. It is however transdisciplinary in seeking to address interdependence and co-evolution between human economies and natural ecosystems. As a result, critical natural capital is prized and protected and ecosystems services are valued and incorporated in cost and benefit analyses. The State will have to plan and decide on the policy space it needs in the course of transition to a Blue Economy. At the same time, on a global scale, agreed multilateral governance tools are a basis of the governance of the Blue Economy and the Blue Economy, by implication, promotes accountable and transparent international ocean institutions in ocean policy governance.

Does the Blue Economy Replace Accepted Ocean Governance Principles?

The answer is no. As a concept, it can only flourish by the application of management principles such as the precautionary approach, the polluter pays principle, a linkage to science, the ecosystem approach, stewardship, compliance and enforcement, the use of tools such as maritime spatial planning and the creation of marine protected areas, and peaceful settlement of disputes. In the Blue Economy, for instance, there is no place for non-compliance of flag states.

Is the Blue Economy a Tool or a Process?

Again, the answer is neither. Maritime spatial planning and integrated coastal zone management tools are imperatives of a Blue Economy in order to estimate and protect the real value of natural resources and consequently are essential tools in the application of this concept. It enlarges the definition of the coastal zones' balance of biophysical, social and economic demands and the dimension of the area and thus enlarges the economic and social remits leading to a much wider spatial area that is sustainably managed.

The Blue Economy is a concept that does not separate the implications and interrelationship of zones but treats the total linkages as interdependent - whether on the High Seas or in the EEZ - a new paradigm in managing human relationships with the ocean.

The Blue Economy concept promotes the long term economics of human welfare as living from the ocean and brings with it changes to outdated concepts: to consider but one example, that of the outdated formula of the Maximum Sustainable Yield (MSY) in fish harvesting. The Blue Economy working hand in hand with the scientific community would enable the assimilation of conservation with ethical use, resulting in reduced "guess work" and as a result promoting greater enforcement and compliance with international or regional agreements. It is about commitment to the future in such areas as fisheries, conservation of high seas biodiversity combined with the protection of life and property at the coast.

Is the Blue Economy a Magic Wand?

The answer is no. It does however require a change of mindset and the acceptance of moral and ethical values in the management of human relations with the ocean and coasts. It is a work in progress as an intergenerational concept of sustainability.

How are Communities and Property Protected in the Blue Economy?

The Secretary-General of the UN on 3 October 2011[8] stated:

"Rising sea levels are a major impact of climate change – and an urgent concern. Sixty million people now live within one meter of sea level. By the end of the century, that number will jump to 130 million. Major coastal cities – such as Cairo, New York, Karachi, Calcutta, Belem, New Orleans, Shanghai, Tokyo, Lagos, Miami and Amsterdam – could face serious threats from storm surges.

---

[8] United Nations Secretary-General Message, World Habitat Day 2011, (*opcit*);

The nexus between urbanization and climate change is real and potentially deadly."

Natural and human-made disasters have been on the rise worldwide since the 1950s, coinciding with the rise in world urban population. As climate change continues to occur, disasters such as landslides, floods, windstorms and extreme temperatures may occur with greater frequency and intensity.[9] Urban vulnerability to climate change will therefore depend upon disaster preparedness, defined as *"activities and measures taken in advance to ensure effective response to the impact of hazards, including the issuance of timely and effective early warnings and the temporary evacuation of people and property from threatened locations."* [10]

In the Blue Economy the general public, private and public sectors, political officials and practicing professionals, all become increasingly aware of the serious consequences that disaster risks pose for their societies. Consequently there will be a growing

---

[9] United Nations Human Settlements Programme, UN-HABITAT: Impacts of Climate Change upon Urban Areas; in the Series: Global Report on Human Settlements, 2011, Cities and Climate Change, page 65;

demand for education to spur the better management and anticipated reduction of those risks. Reducing disaster risks is a multi-dimensional problem requiring a multi-dimensional solution; science and technology alone cannot achieve the ultimate results.

The Blue Economy embraces the intrinsic value of traditional methods and indigenous knowledge. However, in order to be effective, adequate allocation of resources must be dedicated to building up resilience through capacity building particularly in developing countries. The Blue Economy is about integrating the contribution of the productive sectors through benefit sharing as the only feasible way to meet the needs of society for disaster risk reduction and human sustainability. It is relevant to note that the UN Office for Disaster Risk Reduction (UNISDR) reported in May 2013[11]:*"While noting that almost 90% of countries report the integration of disaster risk reduction in some form within public investment and planning decisions, the*

---

[10] Briceno Salvano A: 2008: Today's Education for Tomorrow's Disaster Risk Reduction; in Risk Wise, Tudor Rose, P. 14-17;

report also finds that a key challenge is finding the resources to ensure that frameworks and principles become operational."

Is the Blue Economy a Licence for the Productive Sector to Exploit Resources with Impunity?

This answer is a definite *"no"*. One outstanding example is the precarious balance between the health of the ocean and the sustainable use of its resources. Fisheries are an example of human mismanagement, greed[12] and policies *beyond reason*. The worrisome and unforgivable state of global fish stocks and fisheries is a result of human arrogance embedded in the greed of unsustainable overfishing, destructive practices, bottom and seamount trawling, Illegal, Unreported and Unregulated (IUU) fishing and piracy, non-compliant flag states, immoral and wasteful discards and by-catch, overexploitation and depletion of species through

---

[11] United Nations Office for Disaster Risk Reduction (UNISDR): Press release 23 May 2013; *http://www.unisdr.org/archive/33319* (accessed 4 June 2013);

[12] Behnam A.; Statement on the launch of the publication - the World Ocean Review (2); The Future of Fish – The Fisheries of the Future; Hamburg, Germany, 21st February 2013;

subsidies, unfair and inequitable access agreements and public complacence public through lack of awareness and unfettered consumption.

The situation may not be in all cases reversible but it is not irreparable as the publication: World Ocean Review 2: "The Future of Fish – The Fisheries of the Future"shows.[13] The policies of reason which are at the heart of the Blue Economy aim at achieving long term sustainability and generational security by placing an economic price on noncompliance to be incorporated in the economic and financial management of ocean resources within and beyond national jurisdiction.

---

[13] The Future of Fish – The Fisheries of the Future: WOR 2; 2013, ISBN 978-3-866482005; download from: *http://worldoceanreview.com/en/wor-2/*

LUMEN

PART THREE

What Has Changed and What Needs to Change: From UNCLOS to RIO+20 and the Ocean Compact

In 2012 the international community celebrated the 30th anniversary of the opening for signature of the United Nations Convention on Law of the Sea (UNCLOS). There was no doubt in the minds of most of those who had celebrated its entry into force that it was one of humanity's great achievements to have adopted a universal constitution for the governance of the ocean.

Until thirty years ago human relationship with the ocean was governed by a philosophy that was devoid of moral or ethical dimension. *Mare Liberum*[1] or what is known as the traditional regime of the

---

[1] *Mare Liberum* (Freedom of the Seas) a concept formulated in 1609 by Dutch jurist and philosopher Hugo Grotius as a principle of international law, thus that the sea was international territory and all nations were free

high seas was based on a principle conceived at the time by pirates to serve piracy - designating ocean space for eternal plunder under a false premise of limitless and inexhaustible resources.

Unlike the *Mare Liberum* regime that dominated the governance of the ocean for centuries, UNCLOS was underpinned by an ethical and moral dimension framing the respect for common goods and upheld the principle of the common heritage of humankind and the equitable and peaceful use of ocean services and resources. UNCLOS was heralded as a model for a new international order.

In the thirty years since the adoption of UNCLOS, a plethora of complex governance architecture has been developing in support of UNCLOS ranging from protocols, conventions, binding and non-binding multilateral agreements, guidelines, model rules etc. throughout the United Nations system and the multiples of regional arrangements.

---

to use it for seafaring trade. *http://en.wikipedia.org/wiki/Mare_Liberum* (accessed 21 May 2013);

However, UNCLOS and the related paraphernalia of instruments did not guarantee implementation through enforcement and compliance. Despite all good intentions and expressed good will by all stakeholders our oceans are in deep trouble. The human imprint on the ocean has been destructive and unconscionable. At the same time nations have failed to protect property and life from the might of the ocean's natural impact on human settlements, an impact that has been further aggravated by humankind's impact on climate change.

Since the adoption of UNCLOS a stark governance deficit has evolved for the sustainable management of humankind's interaction with the oceans. Thirty years since the adoption of the sole constitution of the ocean, advances in knowledge and innovation have created an additional burden on implementation and enforcement.

In addition systemic issues have remained unresolved within UNCLOS such as the scope of application of the common heritage principle and flag state effective exercise of duties and jurisdiction in the absence of the genuine link, as well as the lack of clarity in the application of the rule of law in areas beyond national jurisdiction on the high seas. In fact, purely in terms of effective governance, the areas of the ocean beyond national jurisdiction suffer the largest governance deficit.

The governance deficit is implicit in the report of the United Nations Secretary-General, he recalls that the water column on the high seas falls under the regime of the freedom of the high seas and any obligation to protect, conserve, and manage living resources and the marine environment fall under the duties of the flag States. [2]

For more than forty years the international community has turned a blind eye to the fact that most Flags of Convenience States or Open Registries are either not willing or incapable of exercising any form of jurisdiction or control over vessels flying their flag. The less reputable ones do not even know of the existence of vessels under their flag.

---

[2] Behnam A; Biodiversity of the Ocean, A Question of Governance, (*opcit*), page 70 *opcit;* reference to UNSG Report (A/60/63/Add.1): Oceans and the law of the sea; Report of the Secretary-General; Addendum:
http://daccess-dds-ny.un.org/doc/UNDOC/GEN/N04/464/58/PDF/N0446458.pdf
(accessed 31 May 2013);

There are over 2,900 such fishing vessels plundering the sea and carrying out IUU fishing. It has become evident that Port State control, unlike in maritime trade, does not work because in fishing the act is the problem and not the condition of the ship. Furthermore, such vessels often resort to fish laundering on the high seas.[3]

The absence of a mandatory but defined genuine link in UNCLOS and fruitless efforts since to mandate such genuine links, has allowed this chaotic and dangerous situation to develop.

From the state of the health of the ocean it is clearly evident that humans have failed *to live with the ocean and from the ocean, in a sustainable relationship* although the economic and social welfare of humankind depends to a large degree on the oceans' productive sectors and services. The manner in which humans exploit those resources and services has been anything but humane. Over-exploitation and depletion of living resources, compounded by land-based and seaborne pollution, have resulted in the current scarcity of affordable

---

[3] Behnam A; Biodiversity of the Ocean, A Question of Governance, (*op. cit.*);

protein and is making a mockery of attempts to achieve the MDGs relating to health and poverty eradication.

The deteriorating health of the ocean, the over exploitation of its living resources, the irreparable damage to its biodiversity and the new and emerging challenges of climate change as well as the governance deficit particularly on the high seas were on the minds of many concerned stakeholders as the Rio+20 Summit on Sustainable Development approached. There was much expectation from this Third Earth Summit particularly as ocean communities contemplated the linkages of sustainable development of ocean and coasts.

At Rio+20 the ocean was on the multilateral negotiations agenda for the first time in thirty years. Also unlike at any other time, the ocean had a strong voice with a dedicated and vociferous constituency.[4] The ocean community as never before used the social media to connect throughout the world. The Global Ocean Forum organized, on the premises of the conference, an unprecedented Ocean Day and

---

[4] The author, A Behnam., was fortunate to have been nominated as a facilitator of the NGO cluster at Rio+20;

strong lobbying was set in motion in favour of the priories of the ocean community.⁵

The NGO Ocean Cluster identified the following key areas that the Rio+20 negotiating text should address:
1. *Commit, by 2015, to: Maintain or restore fish stocks to maximum ecological sustainable yield (recommitment and updating of JPOI 2002) and; Eliminate overfishing and illegal, unregulated, and unreported fishing (IUU) and eliminate environmentally and socially harmful fishing subsidies that cause overcapacity.*
2. *Agree to negotiate an implementing agreement under the UN Convention on the Law of the Sea to protect and sustainably manage high seas' marine biodiversity.*
3. *Commit funding for both implementation and capacity*

---

⁵ Credit goes to Biliana Cicin Sain, President of the Global Ocean Forum for organizing an extraordinary Ocean Day at Rio+20 that brought together the best international experts, leading international organizations and representatives of member States with an extensive programme and an outstanding analytical document, namely the document: Biliana Cicin-Sain, Miriam Balgos, Joseph Appiott, Kateryna Wowk, and Gwénaëlle Hamon. 2011. *"Oceans at Rio+20: How Well Are We Doing in Meeting the Commitments from the 1992 Earth Summit and the 2002 World Summit on Sustainable Development? Summary for Decision Makers"*. Global Ocean Forum. Post Rio+20, IOI joined the Global Ocean financing project for capacity building in areas beyond national jurisdictions (ABNJ); http://www.globaloceans.org/sites/udel.edu.globaloceans/files/Rio20SummaryReport.pdf (accessed 5 June 2013)

building of integrated ecosystem-based ocean and coastal management and adaptation to climate change at national, regional, and local levels.

It should be noted that IOI first called for an implementation agreement of UNCLOS back in 2007 at the PIMXXXII conference in Malta and in many other forums including the UN Informal Consultative Process ICP.[6]

The extent that the overall outcome of *Rio+20: The Future We Want*,[7] related to sustainable development, left much of civil society and developing countries dissatisfied and let down, especially on the broader issues of sustainable development. Thus, the following words were used to describe the outcome of the Rio Summit: *"nothing much was agreed", "not connected to realities", "failure to deliver", "walking out in despair"* or *"reiterating traditional positions"*. As the saying goes *"the best intentions are fraught with disappointments"*.

---

[6] See also Behnam A., Defending Acquired Rights, TELOS, Volume V, Special Edition, Fondation de Malte, 2011;
[7] Outcome of Rio+20, Doc A/66/L.56 (*opcit*) ; http://www.uncsd2012.org/content/

Martin Khor wrote[8]

"The UN Conference on Sustainable Development, more popularly known as Rio+20, to commemorate the 20th anniversary of the 1992 Earth Summit, ended with expressions of deep disappointment from broad sections of members of the media and the environmental NGOs, who saw little new commitments to action in the final text that was adopted by the heads of states and governments and their senior officials.

This was understandable, as much had been expected from the Rio+20 summit, the biggest international gathering of world leaders this year. This is also because the world is facing serious crises in the global environment and economy, thus there were hopes that some decisive actions would be taken, worthy of the 20th anniversary of the original Rio summit, the UN Conference on Environment and Development.

---

documents/727The%20Future%20We%20Want%2019%20June%20123 0pm.pdf (accessed 24 May 2013)
[8] Martin Khor, Executive Director of the South Centre: The Rio+20 Summit and its Follow Up SouthViews; No.19, 17 July 2012, Geneva; http://www.southcentre.org
/index.php?option=com_content&view=article&id=1794%3Athe-rio20-summit-and-its-follow-up-17-july-
2012&catid=150%3Asouthviews&Itemid=358&lang=en (accessed 24 May 2013)

Thus, there was unhappiness and frustration that the hundred heads of state and government who came to Rio de Janeiro were unable or not asked to take decisive actions. There was a sense that the speeches, roundtables and panel discussions at the huge Rio Centro conference centre were part of a ceremonial function for the political leaders, while the tough decisions required by the crises were avoided or postponed."

However, it was not all doom and gloom (the glass was half full) particularly from the perspective of the ocean community because of renewed commitments to the ocean. At last, after twenty years, civil society and UN institutions succeeded in giving a powerful voice to the ocean. The outcome text included recommendations on ending overfishing, taking action on illegal fishing, phasing out harmful fisheries subsidies, protecting vulnerable ecosystems, a commitment to deal with agreements on areas beyond national jurisdiction, and the need for capacity building among others.

Ten out of nineteen paragraphs on oceans and seas related to fisheries, an indication of the serious state of global fishery resources.

The manner in which UNCLOS was reaffirmed was also a reflection of the nature of compromise in the United Nations debates. Para 159 of the Future We Want,[9] states:
"159. We recognize the importance of the Convention on the Law of the Sea to advancing sustainable development and its near universal adoption by States, and in this regard we urge all its parties to fully implement their obligations under the Convention."

Regrettably Rio+20 placed no obligation to those who have not ratified the convention and they remain free to follow *Mare Liberum* - an outdated concept in itself that may be described as a constitution for piracy.

Furthermore, the most disputed and hardest to reach agreement was para 162 on implementing agreement:
"162. We recognize the importance of the conservation and sustainable use of marine biodiversity beyond areas

of national jurisdiction. We note the ongoing work under the auspices of the General Assembly of the Ad Hoc Open-ended Informal Working Group to study issues relating to the conservation and sustainable use of marine biological diversity beyond areas of national jurisdiction. Building on the work of the Ad Hoc Open-ended Informal Working Group and before the end of the sixty-ninth session of the General Assembly, we commit to address, on an urgent basis, the issue of the conservation and sustainable use of marine biological diversity of areas beyond national jurisdiction, including by taking a decision on the development of an international instrument under the Convention on the Law of the Sea."

This highlights the intricate diplomatic layers and bureaucratic tactics in delaying decision-making processes for a clear and globally recognized urgent need to protect our blue planet.

In one area of direct concern to IOI, Para 160 of the Rio text emphasizes capacity building of developing countries for the sustainable use of the ocean and calls for transfer of technology and cooperation to implement the related provisions of

---

[9] The Future We Want, outcome of Rio+20 (*opcit*);

UNCLOS with the caveat ..." *taking into account IOC criteria and guidelines for such transfer of technology."*

"160. We recognize the importance of building the capacity of developing countries to be able to benefit from the conservation and sustainable use of the oceans and seas and their resources, and in this regard we emphasize the need for cooperation in marine scientific research to implement the provisions of the Convention on the Law of the Sea and the outcomes of the major summits on sustainable development, as well as for the transfer of technology, taking into account the Intergovernmental Oceanographic Commission Criteria and Guidelines on the Transfer of Marine Technology.[10]

There is no doubt that such transfer of technology is not as straightforward as wished for by developing countries nor does it open the door to a transfer of technology as was at the heart of the code of Conduct for Transfer of Technology that was under negotiation in UNCTAD in the eighties.[11]

Did *Rio+20: The Future We Want* go far enough?

---

[10] Refers to Intergovernmental Oceanographic Commission, document IOC/INF-1203

[11] United Nations Conference on Trade and Development, UNCTAD, History of, 1964-1984, UNCTAD/OSG/286, page 158-168, UN, New York, 1985;

Not at all; although, given the enormity of current challenges it was a step in the right direction. Undoubtedly civil society wished for much more.

Sue Lieberman, director of International Policy for the Pew Environment Group stated: [12]
"It would be a mistake to call Rio a failure, but for a once-in-a-decade meeting with so much at stake, it was a far cry from a success.
We came to Rio with high expectations for action to address the ocean crisis."

Nevertheless, the High Seas Alliance[13] - which IOI joined at Rio - identified six clear areas for international and national action:
- *"Fulfillment of the UN resolution to end deep sea bottom fishing;*
- *An end to overfishing—including the suspension of fishing in some cases until stocks have recovered;*
- *Requirement that regional fisheries management*

---

[12] The Pew Charitable Trusts: Environmental Initiatives: 2012: Some Progress at Rio, But No Time to Waste: Press Release - Jun 22, 2012; *http://www.pewenvironment.org/news-room/press-releases/some-progress-at-rio-but-no-time-to-waste-85899400661* (accessed 24 May 2013);

[13] High Seas Alliance; Friday, June 22, 2012: No Future We Want Without the Ocean We Need *http://www.oceansinc.org/2012/06/no-future-we-want-without-ocean-we-need.html* (accessed 6 June 2013);

bodies be accountable to the UN;
- *National action to eliminate harmful fisheries subsidies;*
- *Closure of ports to illegally obtained fish;*
- *Establishment of national and high seas marine protected areas, including reserves."*

For the first time in thirty years the ocean was on the agenda of international multilateral negotiations in terms of sustainable development. While Rio+20 fell short of the aspirations of the ocean community it was nevertheless encouraging that not only were commitments to UNCLOS reconfirmed by the contracting Member States but also commitments to other related instruments.

At the same time never had the challenge been so great to the international community to reverse a trend where the harm done to the ocean, if continued unabated, will not allow it to sustain life as we know it. The continued vulnerability of coastal communities to marine hazards and related effects of climate change has become intolerable and a threat to global peace. Rio+20 reconfirmed international commitments for the sustainable development of ocean services and resources however without fundamental change to the *status quo*.

The United Nations Secretary General subsequently delivered on 12 August 2012 an initiative of his own entitled *The Oceans Compact: Healthy Oceans For Prosperity*.[14] This was an unprecedented initiative to set out a strategic vision for the UN system to deliver in a more effective and coherent manner on its own ocean related mandates consistent with the Rio+20 outcome document.

The Compact was in the making well before the Rio+20 documents were prepared. In fact the concern of Mr Ban Ki-Moon, as Secretary General of the United Nations, had been growing as he focused on the achievement of the Millennium Development Goals. He realized that the state of the ocean and the exploitation of its resources were in contradiction with the aim of achieving those MDGs.

On 7 April 2011 the author met with Mr Ban Ki-Moon at the New York UN headquarters and was honoured to present to him a dedicated copy of the then recently launched World Ocean Review 1 (WOR: Living with the Oceans). A product of IOI's partnership with other eminent institutions, the

WOR is the work of a cluster of more than 250 scientists to provide the first independent and comprehensive review of the health and services of the ocean.[15]

In November 2011 the United Nations Secretary-General, through the United Nations Environment Programme (UNEP), appointed five international experts to begin the process towards building the *Ocean Compact* and the author was fortunate to have been amongst the five.

The purpose of the UNSG's *Oceans Compact* was to set out a strategic vision for the UN system to deliver on its ocean related mandates in a more coherent and effective manner, to provide a platform for stakeholder cooperation and to facilitate achieving goals set in a healthy ocean for the prosperity of all.

The stated aim of the *Oceans Compact* is to build upon the range of existing and ongoing activities of the UN system and to assist Member States to

---

[14] UNSG Oceans Compact, (*op. cit.*);
[15] *www.ioinst.org* , Informa 0511, May 2012, IOIHQ/ES05/11;

implement UNCLOS and other relevant global and regional conventions and instruments; the *Oceans Compact* thus addresses a governance deficit that is at the root of our unsustainable relationship with ocean and coasts.

Accepting the *Oceans Compact* will undoubtedly require all stakeholders to upscale their commitments to sustainable actions. It will only be the beginning of the long haul ahead, yet it is humankind's only choice between an infinite cost in the future or a shared temporary burden of a Blue Economy concept which can herald generational ecological sustainability, an efficient use of resources and a fair and equitable social distribution of the costs and benefits of ocean services and resources while contributing to the resilience of communities.

Thus, the *Oceans Compact* while consistent with the Rio+20 outcome document (The Future We Want) goes beyond Rio+20 as it provides goals and objectives in the form of an action plan.

The *Oceans Compact* addresses one goal, that is, the goal of "Healthy Oceans for Prosperity" and three distinct objectives; the very first objective being that of *"Protecting people and improving the health of the oceans"* through a series of proscribed actions.

In the author's opinion and in the hope that the case is not being exaggerated, this objective is as close as one may come to an accurate description of the Blue Economy concept since it puts the human dimension at the centre of that sustainable relationship i.e. *living with the ocean and from the ocean, in a sustainable relationship* compared with the *Future We Want* which focused on *living from the ocean*.

In the *Oceans Compact,* the three inter-related objectives that advance the goal of "Healthy Oceans for Prosperity" are:

1: *Protecting people and improving the health of the oceans through:*
- *Reducing the vulnerability of people to the effects of ocean degradation and natural hazards, including tsunamis, and anthropogenic environmental degradation, including possible sources of livelihood for coastal populations;*
- *Developing ways and means of adaptation to the impacts of climate change, including sea level rise;*
- *Promoting more sustainable management of coastal areas;*

- *Reducing pollutants from sea and land-based activities, including gas and oil extraction, marine debris, harmful substances and nutrients from wastewater, industrial and agricultural runoff entering the world's oceans;*
- *Reducing over-fishing and eliminating destructive fishing practices;*
- *Encouraging a green economy approach in the context of sustainable development and poverty eradication;*
- *Strengthening the implementation of existing agreements.*

In this regard, it is particularly important that:

a. *Regions and countries most vulnerable to marine related hazards (including sea level rise) be identified and mitigation and adaptation plans developed;*
b. *Early warning systems for tsunamis and other extreme events be established for all vulnerable regions;*
c. *By 2025, based on collected scientific data, all countries set relevant national targets for nutrients, marine debris and wastewater.*

2: Protecting, recovering and sustaining the oceans' environment and natural resources and restoring their full food production and livelihoods services through:
- *Rebuilding of over-exploited, depleted and recovering fish stocks, including by encouraging States to renew efforts to ensure that living resources are no longer endangered by over-fishing and destructive fishing practices taking into account the effects of illegal, unreported and unregulated (IUU) fishing;*
- *Conserving and restoring marine habitats important for carbon sequestration and storage;*
- *Conserving and protecting marine and coastal biodiversity;*
- *Halting the spread of invasive alien species; and*
- *Strengthening the implementation of existing instruments and measures.*

3. Strengthening ocean knowledge and the management of oceans through:
- *Promoting marine scientific research,*
- *Strengthening general science-based knowledge and capacity building for ocean management;*
- *Addressing the need for robust ocean observation and relevant infrastructure, including capacity development in ocean and coastal areas;*

- *Deploying all efforts to better understand the effects of climate change on the marine environment and marine biodiversity;*
- *Undertaking further research on, and observation of, the impacts of ocean acidification and supporting efforts to address levels of ocean acidity and the negative impact of such acidity on vulnerable marine ecosystems, particularly coral reefs and mangroves;*
- *Continuing to address with caution ocean fertilization, consistent with the precautionary approach;*
- *Supporting the development of the global integrated assessment of the state of the marine environment including socio-economic aspects by 2014;*
- *Enhancing management frameworks along with coordinated global, regional and national mechanisms to ensure integrated ecosystem management, and protection of coastal populations; and*
- *Promoting the sustainable use and conservation of ocean resources."*

The UNSG makes detailed and extensive commitments of his own to member states, institutions, organisations and civil society in support of efforts and measures to achieve these objectives.

All the proposed measures and actions are laudable and possibly achievable if two elements were to be present. The first is political will and the second is resources. Unfortunately currently both are not present in sufficient quantity and quality to make the immediate, urgent, decisive and dramatic changes required.

For instance the resources for capacity building in developing countries are minimal and cannot make a dent in satisfying actual needs, even if the political will to do so was sufficiently strong. That is why in a Blue Economy way of thinking the international community may finally be motivated to place a true value on natural and freely accessible goods and services. When fishing consortiums pay rents as do land based farmers; when shipping alliances pay tolls for maritime transport along shipping lanes as do the haulage companies and truckers on land, and the extractive industries and pharmaceutical companies pay the true value for contractual obligations for their privileges and free access to resources and ocean services, then might the international community find the resources to protect the ocean itself as well as life and property in support of prosperity.

In ocean areas beyond national jurisdiction (ABNJ) one of many possibilities to contemplate is a nominal levy under the shared benefits of common goods and the common heritage principle, some of which may be allocated to assist developing countries in implementing capacity development polices supportive of the Blue Economy concept. For such a purpose an international entity as the Sea Bed Authority could well administer such a levy.

Understandably, given the current state of multilateral cooperation, such a remedy remains a far expectation; meanwhile the UNSG can only appeal to governments and stakeholders to demonstrate goodwill. The UNSG himself has committed to support all stakeholders and member states by his determination to create an Ocean Advisory Group to bring together different stakeholders and to contribute to developing a new focus and direction for the work of the UN system on ocean issues. In the section *Moving Forward* of the *Oceans Compact* he encapsulated a fresh vision:
"*Changing the way we use the oceans will require changes in many areas including in market and finance incentives such as certification and investor schemes, responsible governance of tenure to marine space, fisheries and coastal land that underpin sustainable*

livelihoods, and environmental, social and governance reporting. But further work is warranted. Developed and developing countries' public and private sectors need to improve their capacity for ocean administration and knowledge sharing, and to promote capacity building. Civil society's capacity to engage in ocean issues could also be strengthened through citizen science, ocean awareness and literacy, environmental citizenship and youth programmes."

A Personal Reflection

While the UNSG *Oceans Compact* aims at ensuring that all stakeholders act with responsibility and reason, and Rio+20 outcomes contained in *The Future We Want* are clear on the matter, the future we want for future generations is our choice, it is in our hands to bestow it to them. However, we are in need of a mindset change particularly to the extent that every individual assumes his or her responsibility and accepts to share in the inevitable sacrifice to bring about an *Ocean Spring*.

We have charted in those two historic documents a clear path to a Blue Economy to ensure a better and more implementable regime of ocean policies and governance, embedded in UNCLOS and mirroring the eternal vision of IOI's founder Elisabeth Mann Borgese, *mother of the ocean*. IOI is her legacy: an aspiration and an inspiration for healthy oceans and universal prosperity.

The ocean community has come a long way since the World Summit on Sustainable Development (WSSD) in Johannesburg[16] when Elisabeth Mann Borgese made her courageous last stand and ensured that the oceans were put on the development agenda, even at that late stage.

We in the International Ocean Institute owe it to her to fully engage in pushing ocean issues to the forefront of humanity's and decision-makers' concerns and in engaging fully with the concept of the Blue Economy.

---

[16] UN Conference on Sustainable Development, 10 years after the Earth Summit in 1992; *http://www.un.org/events/wssd/* (accessed 24 May 2013)

LUMEN MONOGRAPH SERIES

This book forms part of the Fondation de Malte Lumen monograph series.

The Fondation de Malte was originally formed in 1998 through the inspiration of the late Mercedes Busuttil and registered in Malta by Public Deed. The Fondation de Malte is an international NGO, based in Malta, dedicated to cultural affairs, environmental concerns, education and human rights. It acts through the organisation of seminars, conferences, courses and publications.

For subscription, contribution details and to order previous publications, kindly send an e-mail to info@fondationdemalte.org

TELOS SERIES

Volume I
Renewable Energy in Malta
Blanche REUZE

Turkey in Europe?
David Raphaël BUSUTTIL

Volume II
So Farewell, Fishes and Whales
Sidney HOLT

A Footnote on Pierre Teilhard de Chardin
Salvino BUSUTTIL

Malta – Too Many Walls, Not Enough Bridges?
Rebecca FILLETTI

Malte, Europe et les Visas: Les obstacles pour entrer en Union Européenne
Nadege DAZY

A Mediterranean Union : A New Vision for Mediterranean Cooperation
Salvino BUSUTTIL & David Raphaël BUSUTTIL

Volume III – The Fall of the Berlin Wall: Twenty Years After, What Progress?

Marx, a Christian?
Salvino BUSUTTIL

Two decades without ideological competition: Are we winners or are we losers? Some thoughts on the 20th anniversary of the 'Velvet Revolutions'
Janos J. BOGARDI

The Response of the European Court of Human Rights to the Fall of Communism
Giovanni BONELLO

La Chute du "Mur de Berlin" tournant dans la cooperation scientifique et technique entre l'Europe de l'Ouest et l'Europe de l'Est: les perspectives d'avenir
Jean-Pierre MASSUE

A Millenium of Paradox
Awni BEHNAM

Liquider le passé ou oublier le passé, mais sauvegarder la mémoire ?
Karel VASAK

Volume IV – What Future for Future Generations?

De-Platonising the Guardian in the context of the Rights of Future Generations
Peter SERRACINO INGLOTT

Circonstances de la justice et promesses pour les generations futures
Olivier GODARD

Générations futures et urbanisation galopante du pourtour méditerranéen : un défi supplémentaire
Eva RIOLLOT

Rights, Present Duties, Universal Responsibilities
Salvino BUSUTTIL

L'intervento in alto mare fra "non refoulement", diritti umani e contrasto all'immigrazione clandestina
Claudio ZANGHI

Immigration, asile et droits de l'homme en Europe: l'exemple maltais
Mélanie LAUDRIEC

Volume V
– Special Edition in Honour of Guido de Marco

Foreword
Mario DE MARCO

Homenagem ao Presidente Guido de Marco
Homage to President Guido de Marco
Mário SOARES

The Independent World Commission on the Oceans : A Station in the Life of Guido de Marco
Lucius CAFLISCH

Defending Acquired Rights, The Common Heritage Principle and UNCLOS
Awni BEHNAM

Guido de Marco: Visionary Realism versus Geopolitical Complacency
Richard FALK

Unfinished Business
Sidney HOLT

Biodiversity in the Oceans A 21st Century View
Peter BRIDGEWATER & Ian CRESSWELL

On Breadth and Depth Space for "Ocean Development"
Yiming CAI

An Uncommonly Good Man
Salvino BUSUTTIL

Volume VII
– Food (in)Security in the Mediterranean

Foreword
George PULLICINO

Food Security and Food Safety in the Mediterranean Region. What Role for the European Union?
John DALLI

"Food Security" ed il Mediterraneo
Paolo DE CASTRO

Sostenibilità e Sicurezza Alimentare nel Mediterraneo
Cosimo LACIRIGNOLA

La sécurité alimentaire en Méditerranée: un enjeu de développement régional durable
Jean-Louis RASTOIN

Insécurité alimentaire en Méditerranée, volatilité des prix agricoles, des enjeux partagés en Méditerranée, une opportunité pour des actions concertées ?
Vincent DOLLE

Food Security Policy-Making in the Mediterranean
Justin ZAHRA

Logistique et sécurité alimentaire en Méditerranée
Sébastien ABIS

Food Security, Food Pricing and Tourism in their Mediterranean Setting
Salvino BUSUTTIL

www.ingramcontent.com/pod-product-compliance
Lightning Source LLC
Chambersburg PA
CBHW022112170526
45157CB00004B/1602